STEAM & Me™

GREEN ENERGY

EMMA CARLSON BERNE AND L. J. TRACOSAS

Starry Forest Books

SCIENCE · TECHNOLOGY · ENGINEERING · ARTS · MATHEMATICS

Draw a super-smart robot. Create your own wind energy. Find out if your teeth are as sharp as a shark's. Go back in time to the world of dinosaurs or rocket into space. Power up that scientific brain of yours with STEAM&Me!

Photos, facts, and fun hands-on activities fill every book. Explore and expand your world with science, technology, engineering, arts, and math.

STEAM&Me is all about you!

Great photos to help you get the picture

New ideas sure to change how you see your world

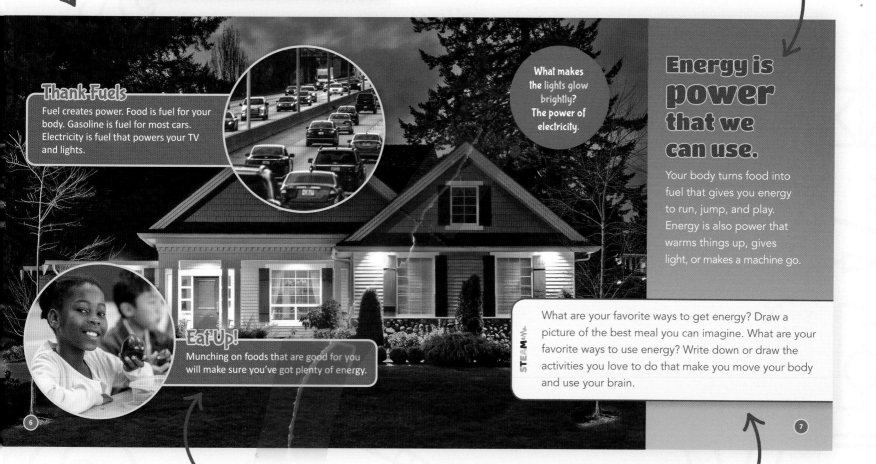

Thank Fuels
Fuel creates power. Food is fuel for your body. Gasoline is fuel for most cars. Electricity is fuel that powers your TV and lights.

What makes the lights glow brightly? The power of electricity.

Eat Up!
Munching on foods that are good for you will make sure you've got plenty of energy.

Energy is POWER that we can use.
Your body turns food into fuel that gives you energy to run, jump, and play. Energy is also power that warms things up, gives light, or makes a machine go.

What are your favorite ways to get energy? Draw a picture of the best meal you can imagine. What are your favorite ways to use energy? Write down or draw the activities you love to do that make you move your body and use your brain.

6

7

Fascinating facts to fill and thrill your brain

Hands-on activities to spark your imagination

Energy Everywhere!

Anything that moves, grows, or powers on uses energy. When you jump out of bed, you're using energy. When you ride to school in a car or bus, that vehicle uses energy. When you switch on a light at night, the light uses energy. When you snuggle under your covers, your body uses energy to create the heat that keeps you warm. In this book, we'll learn about a special type of energy called *green energy*, which comes from natural sources like the sun, wind, water, plants, and Earth. Green energy is all around you!

Power on! Keep an eye out for boxes like this one throughout the book. You'll find ideas for fun hands-on activities that use *your* energy to learn about *green* energy.

STEAM & Me

Think about what energy you use in a day. Point to all the things in this picture that use energy.

Thank Fuels

Fuel creates power. Food is fuel for your body. Gasoline is fuel for most cars. Electricity is fuel that powers your TV and lights.

Eat Up!

Munching on foods that are good for you will make sure you've got plenty of energy.

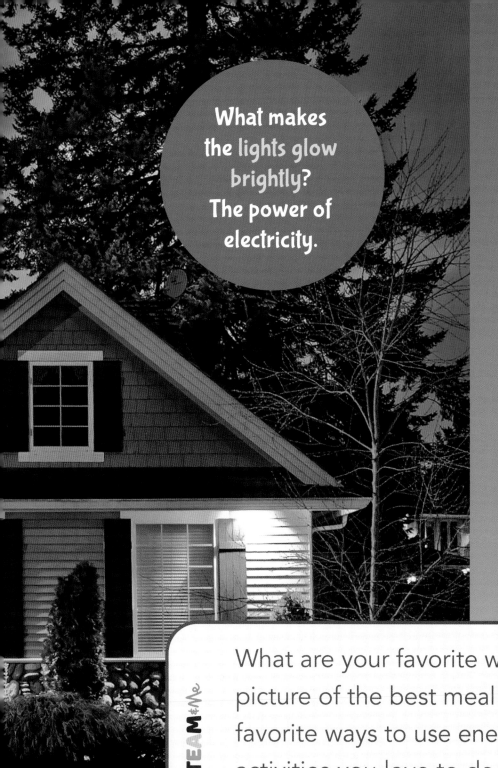

What makes the lights glow brightly? The power of electricity.

Energy is power that we can use.

Your body turns food into fuel that gives you energy to run, jump, and play. Energy is also power that warms things up, gives light, or makes a machine go.

STEAM & Me

What are your favorite ways to get energy? Draw a picture of the best meal you can imagine. What are your favorite ways to use energy? Write down or draw the activities you love to do that make you move your body and use your brain.

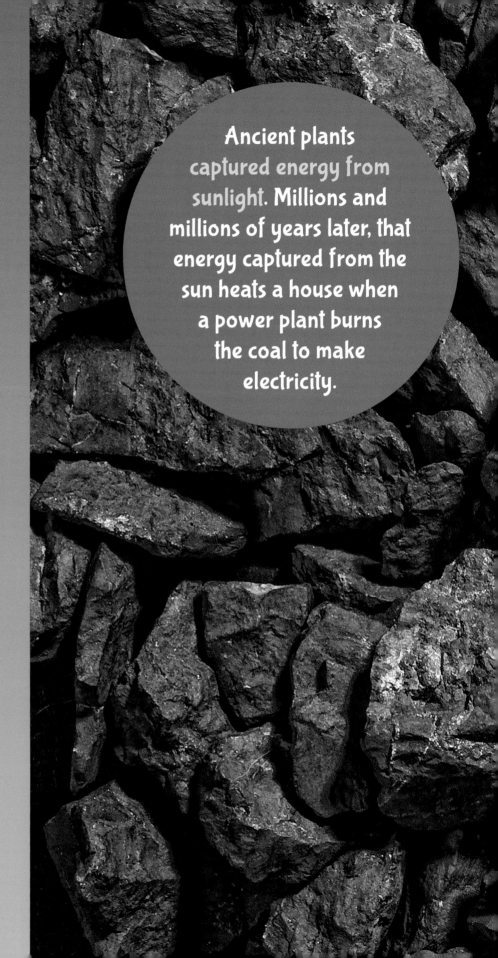

Most of the energy we use comes from fossil fuels.

Do you see grass and plants growing? Over a long period of time, they'll become **fossil** fuels. When a dandelion withers, it falls to the ground. Slowly, over hundreds of millions of years, that dandelion, mixed in with other plant and animal life, gets buried and heated by the Earth. It can then become coal, oil, or gas. We call these fossil fuels because they're old like dinosaur fossils.

Ancient plants captured energy from sunlight. Millions and millions of years later, that energy captured from the sun heats a house when a power plant burns the coal to make electricity.

Cough, Cough!

To get energy from fossil fuels, people must burn them. Car engines burn gasoline to make cars go. Oil can be burned in a furnace to keep a house warm. But burning fossil fuels releases smoke and gases that make air warmer and hard to breathe.

One Time Only

Fossil fuels aren't reusable. Once we burn coal, gas, or oil, it's gone. Remember the dandelion that took hundreds of millions of years to turn into coal? Since fossil fuels take so long to form, we're burning fossil fuels faster than they can be created. So people are looking for different energy sources.

Earth has all the natural resources we need to create green energy. Even plants and garbage can be used to make energy.

Earth has other types of energy, too.

Green energy is energy created from **natural resources** like the sun, wind, water, and heat inside the Earth. Green energy is sometimes called **renewable** energy, because more of it is always being made. The sun rises again every day. Strong winds blow. Rains fill rivers after a dry spell.

Plenty of Energy

People burn fossil fuels for most of the energy they use. But there's a green energy option for almost everything. Kids can even go to schools cooled and heated with green energy.

The SUN is one big ball of energy.

Light and warmth from the sun reach us all the way from space—now that's some powerful energy! The sun's rays provide Earth with light and warmth during the day.

Ready for a big number? 93,000,000—that's how many miles away Earth is from the sun.

How strong is the sun? On a warm, sunny day, take three ice cubes and put each one on a separate plate. Place one plate inside your home under a lamp, place another one in the shade, and place the last one in the sun. Can you guess which ice cube will melt first?

12

Warm-Ups

Reptiles are animals that are *cold-blooded*, which means their bodies don't heat themselves. Instead, reptiles use heat from the sun to warm up.

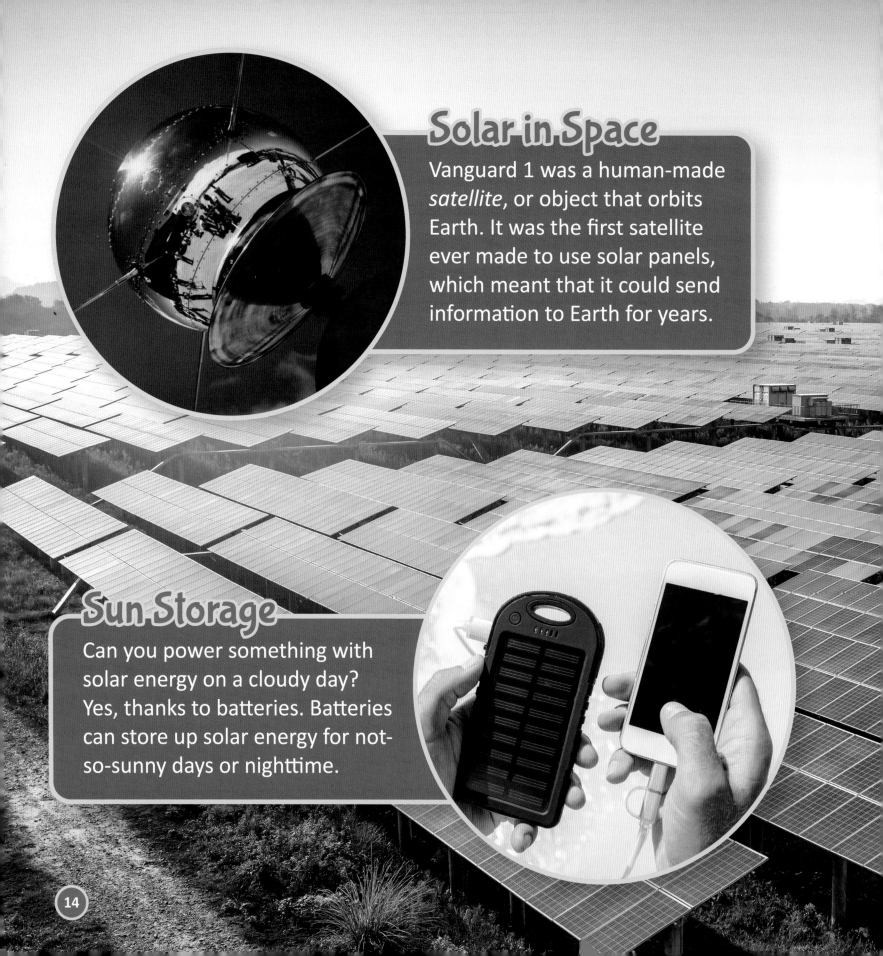

Solar in Space

Vanguard 1 was a human-made *satellite*, or object that orbits Earth. It was the first satellite ever made to use solar panels, which meant that it could send information to Earth for years.

Sun Storage

Can you power something with solar energy on a cloudy day? Yes, thanks to batteries. Batteries can store up solar energy for not-so-sunny days or nighttime.

To collect enough sunlight to make energy for many people, solar panels need to be **large** and **cover a big area.**

Energy from the sun is called *solar energy.*

Solar energy can power watches, calculators, and computers, as well as homes, cars, and buses. We can capture solar energy using *solar panels*: big sheets of **silicon** and silver that absorb the sun's light and warmth and change it into storable, usable electricity and heat.

Green House

Solar panels can be attached directly to the roof of a house.

Wind is created with help from the sun.

The sun's rays warm the air. Hot air rises up, and cooler air whooshes into its spot. That whoosh creates wind. And wind can be powerful. Though average wind speeds are about 9 miles per hour, some storm gusts have set records at more than 200 miles per hour!

Sail Away!

One way to capture wind energy is to raise up a sail. Since ancient times, people have built sailboats. Wind pushing against sails moves boats quickly and quietly over water. Some of the fastest sailboats go about 40 knots, or 46 miles per hour.

Crumple up a clean tissue and set it in front of you at one end of a table. Now blow on it as hard as you can. You're moving that tissue with your own wind energy. Can you use a ruler or a measuring tape to measure how far the tissue traveled?

STEAM & Me

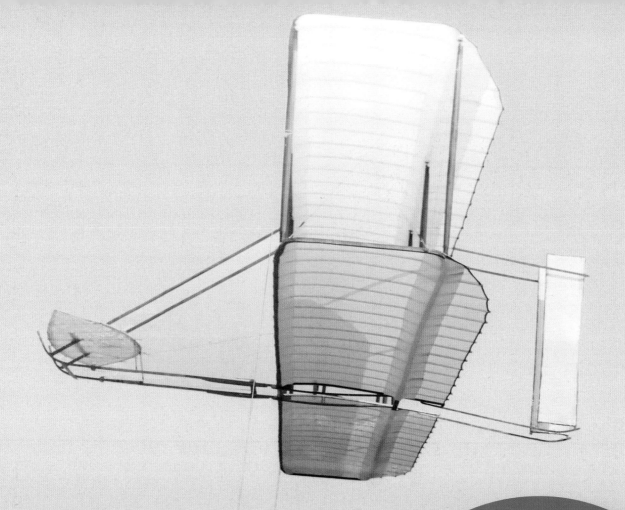

If you've ever flown a kite on a windy day, you've felt the power of the wind! People have used wind energy to fly kites for years. The Wright brothers invented the first airplane. Before they got in and tried it themselves, they tested it as a kite, using two big strings.

Some wind turbines are twice as tall as the Statue of Liberty. Their blades can be 200 feet long or more. When the blades spin, they turn gears that power a generator, turning movement into usable energy.

The same wind energy that rustles leaves and blows your hair can be used for power.

Blowing winds can turn the sails on a windmill, which make a **rotor** go around. People have used windmills for hundreds of years to grind food or pump water. Modern windmills are called *wind turbines*. With special machinery, windmill-like turbines can create electricity out of the movement of the wind.

Wonderful Windmills

Modern turbines are a lot like old windmills. Built in 1740, the Kinderdijk windmills pumped water to stop flooding in the nearby Dutch town.

STEAM

Run with a pinwheel. Did its sails turn? When you run, the wind's energy is moving the pinwheel's sails. In a turbine, the round-and-round movement of the pinwheel would turn gears on a machine, and that machine would create power.

Water has power.

Have you ever seen a waterfall? All that flowing, crashing water is very powerful. *Hydroelectricity* is electricity created by moving water. *Hydro* is Greek for water. To make energy from rushing river water, people designed dams. A *dam* is a structure that holds back the water in a river, then lets some of the water flow through a big propeller that's like a wind turbine. The turning turbine makes electricity.

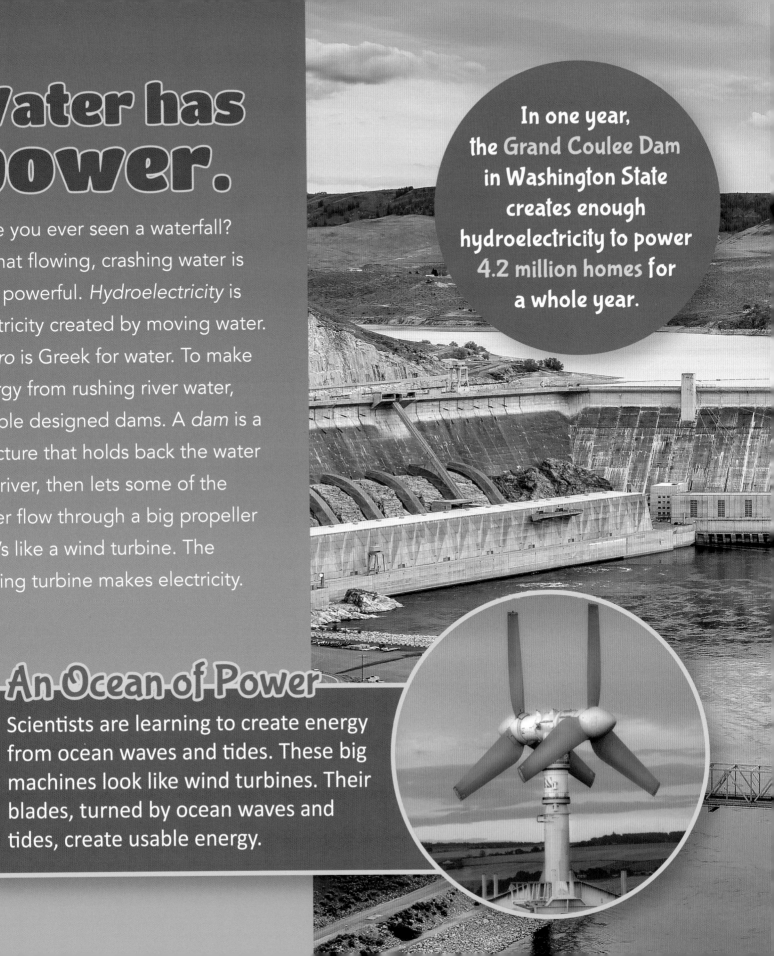

In one year, the Grand Coulee Dam in Washington State creates enough hydroelectricity to power 4.2 million homes for a whole year.

An Ocean of Power

Scientists are learning to create energy from ocean waves and tides. These big machines look like wind turbines. Their blades, turned by ocean waves and tides, create usable energy.

Rushing Rivers

Waterwheels are like windmills powered by flowing water. Ancient people built wheels that rotated under moving water. The wheels turned the water's energy into power that could grind grain.

There is energy in things that grow and that rot.

The energy stored up in plants and animals is called *biomass*. Think about the warmth from a crackling fire. When wood is burned, it releases its biomass energy and makes heat. Burning wood and other biomass can cause pollution, but there are other ways to get energy from biomass that are better for the planet.

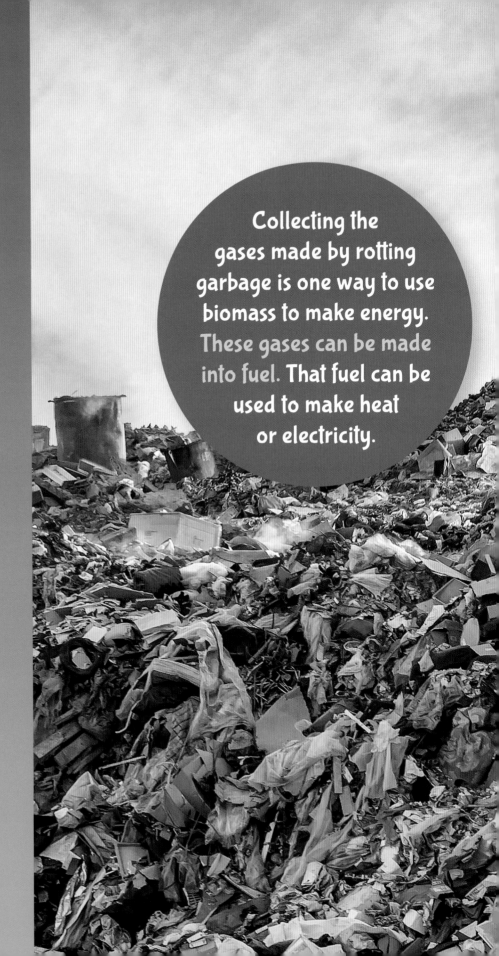

Collecting the gases made by rotting garbage is one way to use biomass to make energy. These gases can be made into fuel. That fuel can be used to make heat or electricity.

Gross Gas!

When human waste and animal waste—that's poop—rots, it releases a gas. This gas can be captured by machines. Then the gas can be used to make heat and electricity.

There's energy in the center of Earth, too.

Earth is made up of three main layers. People live on the outermost layer, called the *crust*. The middle layer is called the *mantle*. At the center of Earth is its *core*, like the core of an apple. But this core is super hot! Scientists think Earth's core is 10,800°F. That's as hot as the surface of the sun. Heat from Earth's core moves outward through the mantle and crust.

Mega-Hot Magma

Heat from Earth's core makes its way up to the crust in the form of *magma*, or melted rock. When magma hits the crust, we call it *lava*.

Gushing Geysers

Geysers spurt water and steam from boiling hot springs heated up by Earth's core. The geyser Old Faithful is called that because it erupts dependably every 60 to 110 minutes, spraying water and steam as high as 184 feet for up to 5 minutes.

These are
the layers of Earth.
Core: iron and magma
Mantle: filled with
magma and rock
Crust: We live
here!

Crust

Mantle

Core

Snow monkeys in Jigokudani Monkey Park in Japan enjoy geothermal energy in the form of a nice warm bath. Snow monkeys keep warm in hot springs.

You can inflate a balloon with hot water. Put a deflated balloon over the mouth of an empty 2-liter plastic bottle. Have a grown-up put some very warm water in a shallow baking pan or bowl. With the grown-up's help, submerge the bottom of the bottle in the warm water. What happens to the balloon?

STEAM&Me

Energy that comes from Earth's heat is called geothermal energy.

In Earth's rocky crust, there are some pools of water that are heated by geothermal energy. The pools of water can be on Earth's crust, like hot springs, or they can be deep underground. Just like steam escapes from a boiling teakettle, hot water and steam can escape these underground water pools. We can use the hot water and steam from these pools to warm homes directly, or to move turbines that can turn movement into energy.

Full Steam Ahead!

Iceland has a lot of underground geothermal activity. In some places, people enjoy swimming in hot springs. In others, big power plants like this one use steam to create electricity. Most buildings in Iceland are heated with geothermal energy.

Green energy can be stored, or saved.

One way to store green energy is to save it in batteries. Just like a battery stores energy to power a toy robot so that it will move when you switch it on, a battery can save up solar energy so it can be used on a cloudy day. *You* can also save energy.

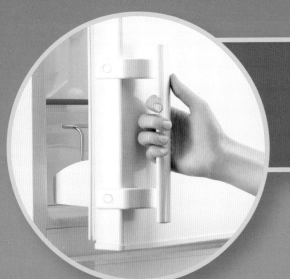

Close It!

Keep doors closed when you're using power. This includes your refrigerator. Save that energy!

Don't Waste!

Time your showers and turn water off when you're brushing your teeth. Every little bit helps.

If you turn toys off when you're done playing, the batteries will last longer.

Energy race! Choose one room in your house. It could be the kitchen, the bathroom, or your bedroom. Set a timer for one minute or ask a grown-up to time you. When the timer starts, count how many things in the room use electricity. When the timer beeps, you're done! How many things did you count? How many can you turn off when you leave the room?

Energy really is everywhere! Where can you find it?

Think about where you live. Is it hot? Windy? Is there a lot of rain? Are you near the ocean? What type of green energy could you use from the natural resources near your home? What are some things your family could do to save energy or use less of it? Try making posters or reminder notes about saving energy in your house.

Glossary

Learn these key words and make them your own!

fossil: a part or print of a plant or animal from long ago, found in earth or rock. *The fossil she found was a dinosaur bone.*

natural resource: something humans use that is found in nature. *Water is a natural resource that we use for many things, like drinking, cooking, and creating energy.*

renewable: can be replaced by nature. *Solar power is renewable because it can be refreshed and resupplied.*

rotor: in an electrical machine, the part that turns. *The windmill's rotor goes around and around when the wind blows.*

silicon: a chemical element that is one of the most common on Earth and is used in many electronics. *Computer chips, lasers, and solar panels all use silicon.*

STEAM & Me and Starry Forest® are trademarks or registered trademarks of Starry Forest Books, Inc. • Text and Illustrations © 2020 and 2021 by Starry Forest Books, Inc. • This 2021 edition published by Starry Forest Books, Inc. • P.O. Box 1797, 217 East 70th Street, New York, NY 10021 • All rights reserved. No part of this publication may be reproduced, stored in a retrieval system, or transmitted in any form or by any means (including electronic, mechanical, photocopying, recording, or otherwise) without prior written permission from the publisher. • ISBN 978-1-946260-88-8 • Manufactured in China • Lot #: 2 4 6 8 10 9 7 5 3 1 • 03/21

ASP: Alamy Stock Photo; IS: iStock; SS: Shutterstock. Cover, Stockr/SS; 5, lisegagne/IS; 6, (UP) ppeterv/IS; 6, (LO) FatCamera/IS; 6-7, karamysh/SS; 8-9, Zhukov Oleg/SS; 9, nampix/SS; 10, Rudmer Zwerver/SS; 10-11, xtock/SS; 11, Steve Mayes/Atkins/ASP; 12-13, NASA/Solar Dynamics Observatory; 13, Joseph Scott Photography/SS; 14, (UP) NASA; 14, (LO) Dmitry Galaganov/SS; 14-15, gyn9038/IS; 15, zstock/SS; 16, Pavel Nesvadba/SS; 17, RGB Ventures/SuperStock/ASP; 18, majeczka/SS; 19, freeartist/ASP; 20, Michael Roper/ASP; 20-21, Nadia Yong/SS; 21, Baciu/SS; 22-23, vchal/SS; 23, LightCooker/SS; 24, (CTR) beboy/SS; 24, (LO) Edward Fielding/SS; 25, Rost9/SS; 26, BlueOrange Studio/SS; 27, njaj/SS; 28, (CTR) Andrew Rafalsky/SS; 28, (LO) Dmitry Kalinovsky/SS; 29, Rawpixel/IS; 30, (UP) Baciu/SS; 30, (CTR) Nadia Yong/SS; 30, (LO) Pavel Nesvadba/SS; 31, (UP LE) Rudmer Zwerver/SS; 31, (CTR LE) FatCamera/IS; 31, (LO LE) Solar Dynamics Observatory/NASA; 31, (UP RT) Dmitry Kalinovsky/SS; 31, (CTR RT 1) Edward Fielding/SS; 31, (CTR RT 2) gyn9038/IS; 31, (LO RT) nampix/SS; 32, (CTR) Zhukov Oleg/SS; 32, (LO) ollo/IS; Back cover, (UP) BlueOrange Studio/Shutterstock, (LO LE) Baciu/Shutterstock, (LO CTR) gyn9038/iStock